MARKET GHOST STORIES

MERCEDES YAEGER

Market Ghost Stories
2020 Seattle Edition

Copyright © 2009 Market Ghost Tours
Edited and reprinted 2020
Published by Mercedes Yaeger
Edited by D.H. Cass Magnuski
Additional edit by Caleah Dean

ISBN 978-0-615-32492-0
Printed in the USA

FOREWORD

I got married at the restaurant, Il Bistro, in Post Alley. Our wedding followed the route of the ghost tours I had given in Pike Place Market. At the Alibi Room, in the basement, our wedding party ate cake and drank champagne. We had our first dance, as husband and wife, to an Irish folk song at Kells Pub. I celebrated the most significant day of my life among the souls that I write about in this book.

In 2016 another soul joined to the ethereal population of the Pike Place Market. My father, Michael Yaeger, passed away. Death felt close to me in ways I had never experienced. Two years later I handed over the creative content and my research into the ghost stories to Unexpected Productions. They now run a theatrical walk telling the stories at night out of the Market Theater.

There have been many changes in Pike Place Market since I originally wrote this book. An expansion that connects the market with the waterfront, replacing the collapsed Municipal Market, was completed. Shops have opened, closed, or moved. I opened my own business in Post Alley, Ghost Alley Espresso, in 2012 and have since sold it.

Ghost Alley Espresso.

When I opened Ghost Alley Espresso, it was clear that something or someone was present there. When securing anything to the east wall of the shop I would use wire as well as nails—wrapping the wire both around the nail and any painting or fixture I put up—because things would fall or even fly off the nails. Electronics in the shop proved problematic and still do today. The iPad, register, and espresso equipment would often behave as though someone unseen was interacting with them. The shop is routinely cleansed with sage and mediums hired to talk to the spirits.

Arthur Goodwin, one of the market's first managers and a designer of the buildings, had his office close to Ghost Alley Espresso. Arthur designed the interior of the market to look like a theater. If you look up while walking in the arcade near Pike Place Fish, you will see thousands of round theatrical lightbulbs lining the ceiling. You may also start to notice the decorated pillars and columns throughout the market.

Arthur may be only one of many ghosts that haunt Lower Post Alley, but he is the one that makes himself most known. Baristas at Ghost Alley Espresso have felt the presence of a man in the shop. One barista, while closing up, saw the apparition of a tall man in a hat standing in the doorway. Arthus Goodwin was famous for his black top hat that he wore almost everyday in the market.

I received an email containing a drawing done by a young girl who had visited Ghost Alley. The email explained that the drawing was of a male figure that the girl had seen inside the shop. The man had wings and wore a dark suit and top hat. A cage stood close to him. Her explanation was that "he was trapped" and that the wings she drew indicated he was an angel.

Drawing by a young visitor to Ghost Alley Espresso.

Because the shop is built into the attendant's room of a 1908 men's bathroom, it was a place Arthur would have frequented daily. Perhaps he had his shoes shined or picked up a newspaper and sat in the window. It is easy to imagine all of the reasons that space would give his soul comfort and, with the dedication he had to the Pike Place Market, it is also easy to imagine him connected to the buildings he helped design—an angel in the Pike Place Market's history.

Arthur Goodwin's pillars and arcades still stand 113 years since the inception of the Pike Place Market. The market has survived threats to tear it down and rapid development on all sides of it. It remains an incubator of small businesses, like the one I started.

I'm writing this foreword in 2020 while in quarantine. Covid-19 is spreading throughout the world, disrupting communities, killing citizens, and crushing small businesses. This summer the market was the most empty it has ever been in its history. The parallels with the Flu Pandemic of 1918 are striking: rapid transmission of the illness, crippled economies, and families making sacrifices in so many ways.

The protests throughout Seattle this year have drawn attention to systemic racism and Seattle's history. Speakers at the rallies have frequently started by acknowledging the ancestral land that Seattle is built on. Posts on social media about the protests tag Seattle as "Occupied Duwamish Territory" or "Ancestral Salish Land." The Mayor and public officials have adopted the call and have also started their public addresses with recognition of the land Seattle stands on. The land that the market is on is especially important to the history of Seattle. It was a prominent hill overlooking Puget Sound long before the first farmers sold onions in 1907. On the northern hillside there were once two cemeteries. On the waterfront, just below the market, was a center for trade where seven longhouses once stood. Princess Angeline, Chief Sealth's (Seattle) daughter, lived below Pike Place. The history of the land and its inhabitants are woven into the ghost stories of the market.

The Pike Place Market remains an incredible place to discover. I hope that in reading this book you will see it in a new way and support the businesses that make up this unique community.

"Through the soil that is my home,
soil I once held in my palm
like a cloud holds the wind,
I watch each face come to visit.

They stare at me.
I wonder why they stand there,
still as the leaf when the wind sleeps."

Antony Yaeger

Excerpt from the poem, *From this Mound of Earth*

The Pike Place Market is a National Historic District. In the district, you will find fishmongers, day-stall tenants, leaseholders, restaurateurs, farmers, and more than four hundred permanent residents. On an international scale, the market is known as a tourist destination. As the longest continually operating market in the United States, established in 1907, it attracts over eight million visitors a year. Nationally, the Pike Place Fish Market (where they throw the fish) and MTV's Real World have highlighted the market's role in defining the Northwest: hard working and entertaining. It is a valued part of Seattle life with fresh goods, seasonal produce, and artists and craftspeople offering hand-made goods.

From 2003 until 2016 I operated ghost tours in the market district. At night the buildings and the red cobblestone streets tell stories of their own: ghost stories. Many of the ghost stories in the Pike Place Market are related to the land and original structures that have been altered through its more than one-hundred-year history. These stories have been told for generations.

I grew up in the market and have heard these ghost stories since I was seven years old. My father, Michael Yaeger, was the market's honorary mayor, a title given to him by the very first mayor of the market, artist Billy King, and a title officially recognized by Governor Mike Lowry in 1993. The market's first mayor and my father both had a reputation as strong advocates for the merchants in the market, for creating unusual events, and for their cunning wits. In the 1980s, for instance, my father renewed an annual event on Valentine's Day: the Crowning of the King and Queen of the Market. He arranged for the Pike Place Fish Market to throw crabs instead of fish and to present the couple with "The Crabs" as they received their crowns. His humor was laced with sexual innuendo and like many of the characters in the market, he was most loved for his personality.

My parents have had a shop in the market since 1980, Watercolors Fresh Daily, where they sell paintings, prints, and calendars. The first years for us as a family in the market were lean. Back then, the market was entirely different from what it is

Pike Place Market 1973. Seattle Municipal Archives.

today. One of my favorite people was a man nicknamed "Spaghetti Eddie" for his rich dreadlocks proliferating on the sides of his head. Across from my parents shop another character set up a daily easel and drew quick drawings of people. He went by the name "Sketcho."

Some of the personalities in the market are residents living in the former hotels that lined Pike Place since the turn of the 1900s. Many of the hotels were boarding houses catering exclusively to men, with single rooms, bathrooms centrally located down the hall, and a maid or cook on staff. The majority of men arriving in Seattle were headed to work in the timber fields, farming, fishing, or gold mining.

Native Americans had made Puget Sound their home for thousands of years. Exploration to the Northwest brought settlers from all points around the globe. By 1907, when the market opened, it reflected that diversity. Early tenants of the Market came from all over the world. The Pike Place Market has been called the "soul" of Seattle, a term used often by its advocates. The buildings have remained intact despite numerous attempts to tear them down or alter their use. It is people that continue to ensure the market's survival: individuals who are passionate about community, about

independent business, and local farming. Some of
those individuals still remain in the arcades.

The Pike Place Market opened in 1907. In
that year, lung infections and influenza topped the
list as causes of death in the United States. Two out
of every ten people could not read or write, and
most doctors received no formal medical training.
Seattle's male population greatly outnumbered its
female and the Klondike Gold Rush was in full
force.

The market opened on top of a broad hill
above the waterfront in a district filled with hotels.
One block away, graves from the former Denny
Hotel Cemetery had been recently moved.

On top of former cemetery land, The Moore
Theater and Hotel, at Second and Virginia, opened
in 1907 with a gala ceremony. Close to three
thousand people were in attendance.

Celebrating the wealth the city acquired since
the discovery of gold in Alaska in 1897, the opening

included the theatrical production, *The Alaskan* [1], based on the Klondike Gold Rush. During the gold rush, an estimated three hundred thousand people made their way through Seattle.

In 1889, Seattle weathered one of the worst fires in the United States. Most of downtown burned in a fire so hot that railroad lines buckled in the heat. The population rose from forty thousand residents at the time of the fire to more than two hundred thousand in 1907. The city had also started a massive engineering project, changing the entire topography of the region.

The Herculean effort undertaken by Seattle after the fire of 1889 produced a brand new city and an underground that is still in use today. The regrading of Seattle was done in stages and when money was available. The process required building new streets first, at heights up to thirty-five feet, and sidewalks last. For a time in early Seattle, pedestrians were forced to use ladders and stairs to access sidewalks below streets.

---

[1] *The Alaskan* was based on a book written by Joseph Blethen, son of *The Seattle Times* publisher Colonel Alden J. Blethen, who was instrumental in opening the Pike Place Market.

Second Avenue, Seattle 1907. Artwork of Seattle and Alaska.

Denny Hill Regrade. Seattle Municipal Archives.

When money became abundant during the Klondike Gold Rush, new sidewalks came into place, linking streets to buildings. An entire hill has disappeared from the city because of this work. The earth and mud from Denny Hill was used as fill in the streets for most of downtown Seattle. In the Seattle Regrade, more earth was moved than in the digging of the Panama Canal. In a project that massive, things can go awry.

"During the final regrading of Denny Hill, in which the land on which the Seattle Cemetery had stood was lowered about sixty feet, several bodies were purportedly found." [2]

In the world of the paranormal and the energetic, there is a common belief that energy is stored in organic materials and that when you disrupt things like wood, metal, or earth, and especially graveyards, stored energy is released.

The people of the Pike Place Market have a small hill in the northern part of the district that has been claimed as an informal burial site for generations. Many former market "characters" have their ashes in the hillside. One such person is Lois "Mae West" Brown.

Lois was a regular visitor to the Pike Place Market until her death in 1995. She was known for her crocheted beer can hats, to which she clipped feathers that hung at both sides of her face. She lived close to the market in senior housing and everyday she would make her way from one end of

---

[2] Angotti, Laura. "Seattle Cemetery." *Online Encyclopedia of Washington State History*, HistoryLink.org.

the market to the other, visiting friends and staffing shops so that workers could take needed breaks. In exchange for her company and acts of kindness she received many gifts and a few dollar bills. A craftsperson gave Lois the nickname "Mae West" and the name stuck.

Mae West's slow, lumbering walk and long purple skirts meant you could easily pick her out in a crowd. The front of her shirt had flair, with buttons that were obnoxious and sexually suggestive. One of her famous lines in the market was reserved only for men. It went, "One leg is Christmas, the other Thanksgiving. Why don't you visit me sometime between the holidays?"

She was loved so much that May 18th was declared *Mae West Day* in Seattle by Mayor Norm Rice in 1994. Before her death, she had a glorious *Mae West Day* and was paraded down Pike Place in a produce truck filled with cut flowers. It was my father who persuaded the city's mayor to honor her as the Queen of the Pike Place Market.

In 1995, while she was cooking in her apartment, the sleeve of her shirt caught fire. She was burned severely. At Harborview Medical Center, she told the doctor attending to get word to her "friends in the market." News came to the market that a woman named Lois was dying and requesting someone visit her. For most of the community, she was only known as "Mae West." It took a few days for someone to realize Lois was our Market Queen. A craftsperson saw her just before her death. Her last request was that her ashes be scattered in the market. They were scattered at the base of a white plum tree in the Soames Dunn courtyard and remained there, at peace, until 2007.

In 2007, the white plum tree was removed. What was found at the base of the tree proved what many market people argued was reason to leave it in place. It was the resting place not only for Mae West's ashes but for many other people as well. Small containers with cremated remains were found in the earth at the base of the tree. For people in the market, the hillside where the tree stood was an informal graveyard. The tree itself was thought to have been planted by Chief Sealth's daughter,

Princess Angeline, marking the native burial grounds in the original hillside.

After the ashes of Mae West were scattered there in 1995, plums started growing again, a sight not seen in years. People argued that the blossoms of the tree appeared to be purple instead of white. In photographs there was often a purple hue to the flowers. With the removal of the tree, came stories of visitations from Mae West's ghost in the arcades. She is seen walking slowly and occasionally hiding behind pillars. Her spirit leans out around the pillars and says, "Boo." Given her humor in life, it is no wonder that she would take great delight in that.

The tree once shaded Post Alley, which runs throughout the Pike Place Market. The alley earned its name for buildings that were supported by posts, erected on top of the uneven landscape that was originally Seattle. The story that it was once known as "Hitching Post Alley"- where you could hitch your horse for a quick shopping trip - has become one of the legends of the market.

In the southern section of Post Alley there is a pizza restaurant called the Alibi Room. It is inside an old hotel and occupies the original first floor and basement of the building. There are three ghosts inside. The first was even talked about when Bugsy's Pizzeria occupied the space in the 1980s: a man standing at the base of the stairs in the basement of the building who simply introduces himself as "Frank."

During the market's hundred year anniversary celebrations, in 2007, Frank became very active and very visible. Customers at the Alibi Room said that he would not only introduce himself but ask if they needed directions. Since the bathrooms are located close to where Frank was seen, many of the questions he answered were the same as queries the workers in the market get every day, "Where are the toilets?"

Frank Goodwin, one of the market's first owners in 1907 and architect of the buildings, had his office close to the old hotel. His birthday is the same as the market's opening day, August 17th. His entrepreneurial vision had earned him a reputation and wealth in the Klondike Gold Rush. Frank brought a vision for investing in public works to Seattle and he and his brothers were the main shareholders in Seattle's original Public Market.

The very first day the market opened, eight farmers showed up to sell and more than two thousand people showed up to buy. There is an account of a farmer hiding behind his cart and placing a tin can out as the hordes of shoppers overtook his makeshift vegetable stand. The next day, forty farmers showed up to sell.

The Market in 1907. Seattle Municipal Archives

At the height of the market's history, three thousand daily workers showed up to sell along Pike Place, in the arcades, in five levels of retail space below and along Western Avenue.

Frank Goodwin and his family created what we now know as the Pike Place Market. Today he rests in peace in a graveyard, thanks in part to his family's visit, on his birthday, to the bottom of the Alibi Room in 2007. In August 2007, the market turned one hundred years old, the longest continuously operating market in the United States.

Just before the hundred year anniversary, I received an email from a descendant of Frank Goodwin. She wanted to arrange a ghost tour for her family. The entire Goodwin family was planning to attend the celebrations. Right at the same time, the owner of the Alibi Room also contacted me to tell me that Frank had started to show up frequently. I wondered if the two events could be related. The Goodwin family was so large that I gave them two tours of the market. They provided me with scans of original documents and photos and even footage of another relative, Arthur Goodwin, dancing.

Looking down Post Alley, the Alibi Room on the right.

On August 17, 2007, as the rest of the market was celebrating on Pike Place, members of the Goodwin family joined me at a birthday party for Frank Goodwin. We placed a chair by the one window in the lower part of the Alibi Room and toasted the empty chair. We thanked Frank for all of his hard work and sang him Happy Birthday. That day, when the woman who had arranged for the tours traveled home, she found herself compelled to visit his grave-site at Acacia Memorial Park in Lake City. She later stated that she felt as though she was laying Frank to rest. His ghost had traveled with her to his own grave. Frank has not been seen since.

Right around the corner from where Frank greeted people is the kitchen for the Alibi Room. The door to the kitchen is locked at closing and yet workers regularly report they find it open in the mornings, just a few inches: someone or something unlocks it. People walking by the kitchen when the door is open say they sense a longing from inside the room and a feeling that someone is trapped inside.

One psychic reported that she heard a young woman speaking in the Russian language inside the

First Avenue 1916. Seattle Municipal Archives.

kitchen. People on the ghost tour have also heard a woman speaking in a foreign language in the basement of the Alibi Room.

Seattle had a problem early on of attracting too few women to its rugged terrain. One man, Asa Mercer, even attempted to persuade the U.S. Army to assist in bringing women to Seattle. He led two campaigns to the East Coast to woo women westward. "Territorial officials favored the plan. Many of them were handsome bachelors themselves, but there just wasn't any money in the public treasury for such an enterprise.
Mercer decided to put his campaign on a personal basis. He traveled about the area with a highly attractive sales pitch. "Let me have the price of a girl's passage out from the East," he suggested slyly, "and the chances are she'll be so grateful that she'll marry you in a hurry when she gets here...before the rest can start courting her." [3]

While he did succeed in bringing some women to Seattle, his recruits were far fewer than

---

[3] Newell, Gordon and Sherwood, Don *Totem Tales of Old Seattle:* Superior Publishing, 1956.

hoped. His attempts became the fodder for a U.S. TV show in 1968 called *Here Come the Brides*. The few women that did return with him were known as the "Mercer Girls." Some women that came to Seattle were as rugged as the landscape: gold miners during the Klondike Gold Rush, independent business owners and entrepreneurs.

"By the 1880s, Seattle had an honest-to-badness Tenderloin district south of Yesler Way, complete with saloons, gambling emporiums, box house theaters, and innumerable brothels of varying class, from the lower order 'cribs' to the high end 'parlor houses.'" [4]

Prostitution was an important part of Seattle's formative years. Taxing the trade brought in significant revenue to the young city. For independent women working as "seamstresses," a euphemism for prostitutes, a male dominated town offered some freedoms and wealth. In other cases, it created servitude and debt. On the West Coast there was a form of indentured service that consisted of

[4] Pierce, J. Kingston. *Eccentric Seattle*, Pullman: Washington State University Press, 2003.

women from northern European countries who worked in hotels. Hotel owners paid for passage to Seattle and, in exchange, women worked as cooks and maids. It's possible that the spirit in the bottom of the Alibi Room is a Russian woman who was a servant in the old hotel.

It is thought that what you do in life is often what you do after death: daily routines and pursuits. That could be one reason the Pike Place Market has so many ghost stories. They are, in part, the stories of former workers in the area who are simply returning to work. This philosophy helps to explain the third spirit that has been active at the Alibi Room: the hotel owner or manager.

Employees at the Alibi Room say that there is a male ghost in the restaurant who actively keeps things tidy. At night, when every surface has been cleaned and after everything has been put away, a morsel of food or a scrap of paper that went unnoticed in the cleanup will appear placed on a newly wiped surface. One waitress felt very uncomfortable with this, as though she was constantly under scrutiny. She was walking down the stairs toward the kitchen one night and felt something behind her. Expecting to see a coworker at the top of the stairs, instead she saw a man's face directly behind her looking down at her, his nose within inches of hers.

The encounter prompted her to have a cleansing performed at the Alibi Room. Despite her efforts, the ghostly activity continues to this day. Grounded spirits are spirits that are connected to structures or earth. The physical walls of the Alibi Room, the original wood and brick of the hotel, may be the key to why these spirits are still haunting the building.

Another ghost that is seen often in the market is the spirit of Arthur Goodwin, nephew to Frank. He made his way to Seattle shortly after 1907 and is responsible for the interior design of the market. His parents were both actors. Having grown up around the stage, Arthur brought theatrical elements to the market. If you look at the archways, pillars, and

ornate decorations in the Economy Market, you can
see the theatrical influence.

At one time more than 20,000 light bulbs
lined the ceilings of the arcades and were lit up
twenty-four hours a day. The flood of light was a
security measure and a not so subtle competition
with Luna Park, a giant amusement park across
Elliot Bay on Alki Point in West Seattle.

Arthur was known for coming to work dressed
in his finest, donning a top hat as he checked on
vendors. He was responsible for assigning spaces to
farmers and it was said that while he was a horrible
actor, he could mimic any dialect in the market. He
also loved to dance. It was a treat for me to see black
and white footage of him dancing that his
descendants shared with me.

Arthur's office was in the Economy Market at
the corner of First and Pike, on the second floor. It
is in the window to his former office that his spirit is
seen today. In the winter months he is visible
standing at the window with a notepad in hand,
perhaps planning his daily placements.

He is also seen inside the Economy Market, in the Atrium, a huge open space created by gutting the original building. My parents' shop, Watercolors Fresh Daily, is located in the Atrium. The "Dapper Dancer," as my father called him, occasionally graces the interior of the Atrium, wearing a black suit and top hat.

Arthur Goodwin dancing. Courtesy of Kerry Serl.

Through the early 1940s, a dance hall existed on the top floor of the Economy Market, right across from Arthur Goodwin's office. Arthur would attend dances on Saturday nights. That is where he is still seen today, dancing on a dance floor that no longer exists. Those who have seen him say he is dancing in thin air. Interestingly enough, there is a theater in the very bottom of the Economy Market, The Market Theater. They have a ghost they call "Arthur" who also dances on their stage.

Restaurants boast the majority of ghost sightings in the Pike Place Market. Just up from the Alibi Room, in Post Alley, is Il Bistro. It's an elegant restaurant with a sunken bar. In the late 1960s, the space was occupied by three different businesses. The market was a rough place then. Most of it was not in use, and it was known to be dangerous at night. The three businesses included a bar, Boulton's Tavern, which became the Victrola in the late 1960s.

There was a Chinese restaurant, Joe's Rice Bowl, owned by the uncle of former Governor Gary Locke. The Rice Bowl served Chinese food and clam chowder. At the east end of the alley was a notorious bar called the Hideout Tavern. The author Tom Robbins is rumored to have read some of his early writings to people in the Hideout.

Joe's Rice Bowl 1967. Seattle Municipal Archives.

Ghostly activity happens in the space that was formerly the Hideout. Patrons of Il Bistro say that when you sit at a certain table, at the east end of the restaurant, you might have a spectacular view; a woman walking toward you in a white dress. Just as this woman passes the table she walks right into the wall and disappears. She is seen in a white dress gathered at the neck with an open back. She has long hair that flows naturally.

The description of her suggests she may be a

remnant of the Hideout's past. Before the 1960s, it would not be common to see a woman dressed like that in a public space. The bathrooms also have activity. The stall doors slam closed on their own. Additionally, the doors often seem blocked - unable to be opened - as though the stalls are occupied and braced closed. Employees say that even when the bathrooms are empty, the doors can be heard slamming against their frames.

One night, after the death of my father, I was at Il Bistro and I was feeling particularly sad. I was questioning my own research & the ghost stories—wrestling with my own beliefs. I went to the women's restroom & I experienced the hauntings just as people had described. The door to the stall slammed as I entered & when I went to open it I couldn't at first—it was being held closed by an invisible force.

The market was built into a hillside providing five levels of retail space below Pike Place. The lower levels are known as the Down Under. In these levels, shopkeepers and customers have seen the ghosts of children. Some even name them.

Until 2010, a store selling beads had occupied the address of #415 1501 Pike Place. It became retail space after a federal post office in the location was closed due to financial embezzlement by workers in 1973. When former owners of the bead store, Ram and Nina, took on the lease, they inherited the beads, counters, register and the ghost of a young boy. They called him "Jacob."

Nina was the first to notice strange happenings in the shop. At night she organized all the beads into their proper containers. In the morning they would be jumbled up and moved. One day while she was having a particularly emotional phone call, a strand of beads went flying in front of her from a hook on a wall. She felt as though someone was trying to get her attention and her mood quickly changed. An employee of the Bead Zone, which Ram and Nina called their store, described walking through the shop one morning while trying to decide on a necklace to wear during her shift. To her amazement a necklace hanging on a hook flew off and dropped at her feet. As she picked it up she noticed that the blue of the center stone was the exact blue of the dress she was wearing.

When I brought tours into the Bead Zone, I often asked the group to make a request of Jacob to do "something." It is rare that anything happened, but on two occasions things did. Once, two strands of red beads went flying off the wall as though someone had pulled and thrown them. Another time a group of young Girl Scouts asked him to do something and within minutes of the request, the entire room began to smell of wet hay and horse manure. It was so unmistakable that one of the girls asked, "Where are the horses?"

In a short film made by Arthur Goodwin in 1927, there are about five-seconds of footage in which his camera catches numerous young boys lining up on Pike Place to work for the day. They stand with small carts at their sides ready to help customers haul their goods through the market. Other children worked long hours in the stables around the market. Orphaned children found refuge by working for the stable masters. In exchange for their work, they received blankets and hay on which to sleep. Jacob may have been one of those early stable boys remaining close to where he lived and perhaps died.

Number 415 is a challenging place to have a business, not only because inventory keeps being moved around but because of its location and awkward layout. On the north side of the shop is a room that had been sealed since 1973 when the post office moved out. The room is almost as large as the entire shop but with an elevated floor that makes it unsuitable for commercial use. The room was first noticed one morning while the owners of the Bead Zone were parking their car on Western Avenue below. They looked up at the backside of the market and noticed that there were six large windows on the exterior of their bead shop, which was quite strange. Inside the bead shop there were only three. There appeared to be an additional space north of their shop. Anticipating finding that additional space, they knocked on the north wall only to discover that one area sounded hollow.

Upon breaking through the wall they found a large room and the three windows they had seen from Western Avenue. Below the windows were small piles of items. There were piles of beads, piles of pennies, and packets of beads marked with their own handwriting from just a week before opening the sealed space. How all of these things got behind sealed walls remains a mystery.

One Halloween, Jacob's story was in the newspapers in Seattle. The newspaper article made a clever assumption that the beads resembled marbles and that was why Jacob liked them. Young children started to visit the shop with marbles in hand. One child left a basket of marbles for Jacob with a note that read, "These are for you. If you like them, let me know."

The Bead Zone (now permanently closed) moved to a different space on a lower floor. One day two customers were inside that former location standing next to a large table. On the table were containers filled with different colored beads. After several minutes of looking through the containers, they asked Ram if there were any red beads. He told them to look again. When they looked back every container had one solitary red bead in the center. At Number 415 a shop called Merry Tails is now open. The owner has an area devoted for Jacob inside. A small cart and a basket of toys now sit in the middle of "Jacob's Room."

On the third level of the Down Under, you will find an odd wooden ramp that doesn't quite fit in with the rest of the building. It doesn't. It's an old horse ramp that is still visible today. Like worn limbs and aged skin, its wood and uneven surface hint at the decades it has been in use. Photographs taken at the base of the ramp often have orbs in them. Some could be explained as moisture or dust, but there is one solitary orb that reappears in pictures, despite time or season, traveling up and down the ramp. The orb has been seen moving between multiple cameras taking a photograph within seconds of each other.

At least five different ghosts of children have been seen nearby the ramp including a young blonde girl that leads lost children back to their parents. Several people swear they have seen a young boy with brown hair and no eyes. At #319, the ghosts of two small children are thought to be responsible for breaking a glass case that held doll furniture. The doll furniture was found on the floor amongst the shards of glass neatly arranged: pieces stacked on top each other. The owner could not explain this discovery. Every night she used two locks to secure the front door. Neither of the locks had been disrupted, and there was no evidence of a break-in.

In 1999, the Butterworth Mortuary, at 1921 First Avenue, was sold. As they cleaned out the old basement, they found a series of shelves with urns on them, numbered and without names. What little records remained showed that they were unnamed children that died in 1918 and 1919. The Flu Pandemic hit Seattle October 2, 1918, and brought tragedy to the city. Approximately fifty-million people died worldwide during the outbreaks of 1918 and 1919. The illness killed people in the prime of their lives and it was so contagious that public gatherings were outlawed. It killed within days of infection. Those that had to be out in public wore six layer gauze masks. In that year, the city of Seattle also had an outbreak of diphtheria and many children died in that outbreak.

According to health department reports, in 1918, close to thirteen percent of Seattle's population died.[5] During that time, the Butterworth Mortuary would have been very busy. Adding to the deaths was tuberculosis. Seattle's efforts to fight tuberculosis were considered the worst in the United States in 1908 by the US Office of Public Health. Tuberculosis continued to be one of the leading causes of death in Seattle for the next ten years. In 1911, Seattle opened the Firland Sanitarium to treat tuberculosis patients. It remained open until 1973 and was located twelve miles north of downtown Seattle.

At the time of the Flu Pandemic, childbirth and infancy already had a fair share of medical complications and many deaths. A family was

[5] *Department of Health Records 1918*, The Seattle Public Library, Seattle Room.

especially vulnerable if one member caught the flu. Parents risked their own lives if they kept a young child sick at home. During the pandemic, quarantines were set up in hotels around the market. Legend has it that children who are seen in the lower levels are victims of Seattle's Flu Pandemic.

In November 2010, at a paranormal investigation I attended in the lowest level of the market, the sound of children running was heard by the entire group. It was coming from above us. One person went to investigate and found that the area was locked for the night, a fire door and a chain fence secured it. We concluded that no living person could have made the noises. During the investigation, EVP recordings produced a child's voice saying, "I want to catch him." Security guards in the market have also heard the running and the sound of children's laughter in the lower levels.

Underneath the Pike Place Market there is a tunnel that houses two railroad lines. The Burlington Northern Tunnel was built in 1904 and runs south from King Street Station ending just beyond the market's boundaries, on the waterfront at Virginia Street. Construction began in 1903 with two crews digging from opposite ends toward each other. In less than two years, construction was finished. Amazingly, along the route, crews encountered a prehistoric forest preserved in the earth underneath downtown Seattle at Fourth and Spring.

Today, it is not uncommon to feel buildings in the market shake as trains move below. The sound of heavy wheels on tracks and brakes squealing can also be heard in the lower levels. Given its age, the tunnel is grandfathered out of regulations governing similar structures. There are no smoke detectors, no emergency exits, and no lights inside the tunnel. Traveling through it has the potential of being far more frightening than being above. The tunnel may help scientifically explain why people feel physical unrest in the market and especially in the Down Under.

Tunnel below the Market. Seattle Municipal Archives.

There is a barber shop on the fifth level of the Down Under. It was the same small barber shop in the 1940s. In those years, Seattle was a hub of military activity with thousands of soldiers housed around downtown Seattle in former hotels and boarding houses. The market had a lot to offer them: great bars, restaurants, a brothel, and an inexpensive haircut. The problem was that they were often visiting the bars before getting their hair cut. By the time they found the tucked away barber shop on the fifth level, they were a bit sauced and became easy prey for the "Singing Woman Barber." That is the nickname for the ghost that resides in the shop. According to legend, the female barber weighed three hundred and fifty pounds and had a beautiful singing voice. She would sing her customers to sleep and take whatever was in their pockets for herself. She made a nice living doing this.

She was found dead one morning in her shop after suffering a heart attack. The weight of her collapsing body broke the floor below her. When discovered, she was lodged between two levels, with her feet hanging through the ceiling of the level below and her torso and arms lifeless on the fifth floor. It is said that she is still there today, right at the entrance to the shop and that you must guard what is in your pockets or she will reach up and help herself. Her ghost is at the perfect height to do so.

While a very entertaining story to tell, it is really the combination of two stories - that of a barber who stole from her customers, and that of another woman, Beullah, next door to the old barber shop, who did fall to her death and broke the floor below on impact. The two stories have been combined over the years to create the legend that exists today. Beullah lived in the Leland Hotel, located at the entrance of the Pike Place Market. Her stepson, Steve, who shared with me the true story, says that he stills sees her ghost in the window of her former apartment.

Until the early nineteenth century, bloodletting was a common therapeutic practice and barbers offered it as a service. A client would sit in a chair and hold a rod tightly exposing his veins. A barber was responsible for cutting his arms and bleeding him until he fainted. The red and white barber pole still in use today on the exteriors of barbershops was originally a way to advertise the bloodletting procedure.

When the Pike Place Market first opened, it was known as "Seattle's Public Market." The Pike Place Market today includes buildings which were once competing separate markets. The Sanitary Market on the east side of Pike Place was called that because it was the only market into which you could not bring your horse. It was also known for the variety of poultry and meats offered which required that the building, indeed, stay sanitary. My father told me a story about the Sanitary Market when I was young that I sometimes shared on my tour.

During the 1920s, in Washington State, there was an abundance of poultry. The Sanitary Market became the stage for some stiff competition, in which vendors found themselves pitted against each other in selling their chickens. To compete, they created elaborate displays, dressing the chicken carcasses in doll's clothes, and placing small hats on

The Market in 1921. Seattle Municipal Archives.

their heads. According to market old-timers, most of the clothing was made from lettuce leaves. Some merchants created sexual scenes, with chicken carcasses in erotic poses. This time was known as "The Great Chicken Wars of the 1920s."

The market was a robust place for business until World War II. Then things changed. The internment of Japanese Americans on the West Coast forever changed the demographics and uses of the Pike Place Market. At the beginning of the war, two-thirds of the farmers in Washington State were of Japanese descent. When they were forcibly relocated to camps far away from Seattle, the market suffered. While there were still farmers that came to sell, most of the stalls stood empty. By the 1960s, the buildings stood neglected and the mayor of Seattle called the market a "rat trap" and a "fire hazard." A proposal to knock down most of the market was favored by the city.

Through a vote in 1971, the citizens of Seattle decided the market's fate. It was the individual voices of the city and a campaign called Friends of the market headed by Victor Steinbrueck, of the University of Washington School of Architecture, that saved the buildings from the wrecking ball. Initiative #1 prohibited the demolition of buildings within the district and set the stage for federal support in creating the Pike Place Market as we know it today.

Major renovations began, including upgrading the turn of the century buildings and tiling the floors of the arcades. Tiling the floors allowed for people to have a permanent place in the market. For a donation of $35, a personal message or name was cast into each tile. They line the floors today. Some of the tiles have stories of their own.

The Heaven's Gate Cult was established in the 1970s. Led by a persuasive man, Marshall Applewhite, the cult's beliefs centered on the apocalyptic idea that the earth was going to expire. To survive, members needed to leave the earth and the "vessel" of their body. The opportunity to do so presented itself with the comet, Hale-Bopp.

On March 26, 1997, as the comet passed over North America, thirty-nine cult members committed suicide in a rented San Diego mansion. They believed they were boarding a space ship located in the tail of Hale-Bopp. In their pockets, they had three quarters, fare for the trip. A letter left for the owner of the rented mansion where the mass suicide took place stated that the event, certain to be famous, would only add financial value to the property. While the event received wide spread media coverage and the attention of comedians, the house was sold and destroyed.

Heaven's Gate Tile. Photo by Jay Lindberg.

To recruit members to the cult, parties of two would travel to tourist destinations around the United States. Evidence that they were in the Pike

Place Market comes from the tile that they purportedly bought for $35 on June 8, 1985.

The Heaven's Gate tile is located in the North Arcade: Go to the base of Stewart Street where it meets with Pike Place. There you will find the entrance to the Joe Desimone Bridge & the MarketFront building. At that entrance to the bridge, on Pike Place, go to the left & look for the pillar next to the farm tables. The Heaven's Gate tile is just below the first pillar.

The city of Seattle was first established on an island in Pioneer Square surrounded by sixteen hundred acres of tide flats. Seattle had a lot to offer in its early years: a deep natural harbor (one of the deepest in the world) and old-growth timber as far as the eye could see.

Arthur Denny, credited as being one of the first settlers in the region and the founder of Seattle, arrived in 1851. Denny's first choice of real estate, Alki beach, in West Seattle, proved to be a treacherous place to start a city. After spending a

storm filled and tragic winter on the exposed beach,
Denny chose the island across Elliot Bay for his
future city. Then Puget Sound was home to
thousands of Native Americans. Some historians
believe the reason Denny choose an island as the
birthplace of Seattle is because other areas of town
were already inhabited. Waves of epidemics and
treaties moved the native people off their original
lands. By the time of Seattle's great fire in 1889, the
city grew farther north and east, claiming hillsides
around downtown. A year after its inception, Seattle
was chosen by Henry Yesler as the site for a steam
powered sawmill. He founded his sawmill, on what
is today the corner of First Avenue and Yesler Way,
in Pioneer Square. Yesler employed almost every
man in town, including a large number of Native
Americans in the region.

Being a working man's town, Seattle was filled
with brothels throughout downtown. In 1852, the
same year that Henry Yesler arrived, Mary Ann
Conklin dropped anchor in Seattle. She was
married to a Russian sea captain. After he
abandoned her in the Northwest, she helped

establish a hotel in Pioneer Square, The Felker House. The second floor was a parlor house in which Washington was signed into a territory of the United States in 1853.

"When her captain-husband dumped her in Port Townsend following a final rousing row aboard his ship, Mary Ann Conklin was unfazed. Soon after making her way to the ragtag settlement of Seattle, she was running its first hotel with cunning and an iron fist. No mints on pillows at Felker House on First Avenue. When a prissy prosecutor requested a receipt for a space rented for a trial, she flung firewood at him instead." [6]

In her travels, Mary Ann Conklin had learned to swear in seven languages. Sailors going by her house were known to blush at the sound of her cursing from her balcony. She also kept an apron loaded with rocks to throw at people she didn't like. This practice earned her the nickname "Mother Damnable," which stayed with her through her life

---

[6] Paynter, Susan. "She's the mother of all M-Day honorees," *Seattle PI*, May 11, 2007.

and after her death. She was also known as
"Madame Damnable."

She died of old age and was initially buried in
one of Seattle's first cemeteries in Pioneer Square
that flooded regularly. It was not uncommon to see a
body float out with the tide. Hers didn't budge.
When they went to move her to a more permanent
grave-site, they couldn't lift her casket. It took six
men to pull it out of the mud.

In life she was five feet tall and weighed ninety
pounds, so the story goes. In death, her casket
weighed in at 500 hundred pounds.[7] Curiosity led to
opening her casket and finding Madame Damnable
perfectly preserved and ashen in color. Her flesh
had calcified and turned to stone. Supposedly, P.T.
Barnum offered money to buy her remains and
include them in his circus, but the city kept her.
According to some accounts, her body was dragged
up Capitol Hill and buried near the original
entrance of the Lakeview Cemetery. However, there
remains some uncertainty whether Madame

---

[7] Speidel, Bill. *Doc Maynard: The Man Who Invented Seattle,* Seattle:
Nettle Creek, 1978.

Damnable made it all the way to the top of the hill. Some speculate that she is still buried somewhere in downtown Seattle.

Many of Seattle's pioneers are buried at Lakeview Cemetery on Capitol Hill. Among the grave markers for Henry Yesler, Arthur Denny, and Madame Damnable are those for Bruce Lee and his son, Brandon. Their grave-sites receive numerous visitors daily. Tour buses stop in nearby Volunteer Park and tourists walk through the manicured hillsides of Lakeview Cemetery to visit their graves and leave offerings.

The inscription on Brandon Lee's grave reads: "Because we don't know when we will die, we get to think of life as an inexhaustible well. Yet everything happens a certain number of times, and a very small number, really. How many more times will you remember a certain afternoon of your childhood, some afternoon that's so deeply a part of your being that you can't even conceive of your life without it? Perhaps four or five times more. Perhaps not even that. How many more times will you watch the full moon rise? Perhaps twenty. And yet it all seems limitless."

In the mornings, on Pike Place, sometimes a lone shadowy figure is seen walking. It is believed to be the ghost of Brandon Lee. He is seen in the early mornings walking down the cobblestone street wearing a dark cape.

One Madame in Seattle's more recent history took residence in the Pike Place Market by buying the Outlook Hotel, at the main entrance of the market, in 1942. She renamed it the La Salle Hotel after the Cadillac La Salle. Her name was Nellie Curtis and she was a well established Madame in Seattle.

If you stand at the front of the market at night and look at the neon sign that reads "Public Market Center," you will notice that a red light is cast along the side of a neighboring building. It shines and illuminates the La Salle Hotel. That was one way sailors in Seattle knew how to find the

La Salle Hotel. Seattle Municipal Archives.

brothel. The original sign for the La Salle is still visible on the exterior of the building.

In 1942, an outbreak of syphilis in troops housed in Seattle led to the military's request that all brothels in the city be closed. The mayor obliged and closed them down except Nellie Curtis' "La Salle" which stayed open until 1951. The women who worked for her were given business cards that simply read: "La Salle Hotel, Friends Made Easily." Nellie built a set of stairs that ran to Western Avenue below. Urban legend has it that a thousand men would be lined up to get inside the brothel.

"The La Salle was almost too successful," Alice Shorett wrote in the book, *The Pike Place Market: People, Politics and Produce.* She states that one evening, "…there were what seemed to the shore patrol a thousand gobs lined up outside the La Salle, waiting for space in its fifty-seven berths." [8]

When Nellie Curtis sold the La Salle Hotel in 1951, the new owners reported that, by day, seventeen or eighteen men would come to the hotel.

[8] Shorett, Alice and Morgan, Murray. *The Pike Place Market: People, Politics, and Produce,* Pacific Perch Press, 1982.

At night, forty or fifty men would come by, asking where the girls were. The new owners eventually put a sign out at the entrance to the hotel that read "No Girls."

Nellie had begun her business in brothels in the late 1920s at the Camp Hotel on First Avenue. By World War II, she had already saved cash in the amount of $170,000. While operating the La Salle, she was known to keep two rooms locked for her own use. One room contained only men's hats, which she collected. In the other room, cash filled every drawer, box, and shelf. Years later, in 1971, the IRS took her to court for taxes she never paid on cash taken in at the La Salle. They estimated that she owed $172,807.87.[9] While not a ghost, she does live on in "spirit form" today. The Pike Brewery brews a beer in her honor called "Naughty Nellie's Ale."

First Avenue and Pike Street, right at the front of the market, became the destination for prostitutes working the streets in the 1970s and into the early

[9] "Nellie's Place, The IRS vs The World's Oldest Profession" *Seattle P-I*, March 19, 1971.

1980s. During that time, the nickname for First Avenue was "Flesh Avenue" because of the many offerings up and down the street. In 1973, a film depicting Seattle's Flesh Avenue was in major release and up for several Academy Awards. The title was *Cinderella Liberty*, starring James Caan and Marsha Mason. Just as Cinderella had to return by midnight, a "Cinderella Liberty" pass allowed men in the military limited time out on the town. In the film, a sailor falls in love with a "barroom whore" (a term used in the movie) and becomes a father figure to her child.

Seattle was chosen as the location for shooting the film because no sets were required. In the movie, First Avenue is seen in all its glory, with the many night clubs, peep shows, pool halls and bars that lined both sides of the street. One scene takes place in Lower Post Alley where the Gum Wall is located. Across the way was a peep show where the offices for the Pike Place Market management are today.

The movie poster reads: "She's 32. She drinks too much. She hustles pool. She's got a different

First Avenue 1975. Seattle Municipal Archives.

boyfriend every night. She's in trouble. And he's in love." At the end of the film, James Caan boards a greyhound bus to chase his love interest after she has left the city, abandoned her son, and traveled to New Orleans with another man.

The public solicitation of, and relative tolerance toward, prostitution that existed in the 1970s changed in the early 1980s. The market was going through a major restoration supported by federal dollars, and the bodies of young female prostitutes were turning up in the Green River, south of downtown Seattle.

The first bodies, victims of the Green River Killer, were found by a man fishing with his son in 1982. Three bodies were found. Two were floating in the Green River and one was under a bush to the side. All three had been raped repeatedly and strangled. That was the beginning of one of the most terrifying times in Seattle's history. Prosecutors had very few leads in the case and the two possible suspects had both passed polygraph tests. One of the suspects, until he passed the polygraph test, was Gary Ridgeway. He was released after questioning. The killings continued.

It wasn't until 2002, twenty years after the first victims were found, that the killer was brought to justice. By using DNA evidence and technology that was newly available, Gary Ridgeway was finally tried and convicted. He confessed to forty-seven murders, but claims he killed close to seventy women. He considered it his "profession." Gary Ridgeway had been married twice and had a son. He would lure women into his truck by showing them pictures of his son.

In his first murders, he left his victims exposed to the elements so that he could return and have encounters with their corpses. He eventually buried his victims to control that habit. Two years after the first bodies were discovered, a letter was sent to a *Seattle Times* writer that described the Green River Killer's identity. It gave exact details about the car, job and methods of the man who was the killer. The letter was considered fake. It was not. Gary Ridgeway had written the letter. One of his youngest victims was picked up at First and Pike, at the front of the Pike Place Market.

Seattle has had its share of serial killers. Gary Ridgeway and Ted Bundy are the most famous, but there is another killer in Seattle's past. It can be

Doctor Hazzard.

argued that the first serial killer in the Northwest was a woman, Doctor Linda Burfield Hazzard.

In the early 1900s Doctor Hazzard held a degree in fasting and wrote a book boasting of the miraculous effects fasting (starvation) had on all illnesses. The few patients who survived her treatments earned her an exceptional reputation. She took out advertisements in newspapers around the country and attracted patients from as far away as England. Other doctors throughout the country supported the notion that fasting could cure illness. Wealthy patients sought natural cures and would travel to isolated locations in search of whatever fad diet or treatment was popular at the time. Little was known about illness in the early 1900s; doctors were rarely licensed, and few attended any formal schooling.

Doctor Hazzard lived in Seattle with her husband and published her book, *Fasting for the Cure of Disease* in 1908. In it she argues that the cells of the body are in a constant state of producing toxins and that disease is cured through restricting this process.

"Rationally, the method to be employed should remove the cause of the condition, and the first step in its accomplishment is found in the absolute withdrawal of food. The next step taken is the removal of all traces of food rubbish that remain in the intestines, and this should be done with the utmost celerity. Warm water enemas of plain water properly given will flush the colon, and before the first day is ended, the major portion of the mass of poisonous filth will have been removed." [10]

While working in Seattle, she conveniently housed some of her first patients in hotels close to the city's first mortuary. The Butterworth Mortuary was located in what is now the Pike Place Market district. She was a devoted care giver, feeding her patients a weak soup made from tomatoes twice a day and giving them vigorous massages to rid the body of toxins. They also received three enemas daily. As the patients became weaker, the enemas would last two and three hours to rid the body of

---

[10] Hazzard, Linda Burfield. *Fasting for the Cure of Disease*. Seattle: WA Harrison Publishing, 1908.

even more toxins. Within months many of her patients were emaciated piles of bones.

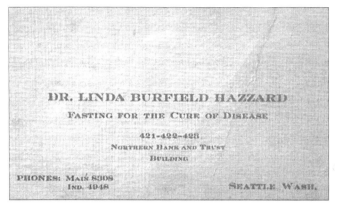

Original business card belonging to author Gregg Olsen.

Many of them were wealthy. As her patients became frail in body and in mind they were easily convinced that they would fall prey to the greed of relatives. She would protect their holdings and when they were healthy (by her assurances they would be) everything would be returned. Rarely did they recover and their money, land, and personal items became the property of Doctor Linda Hazzard.

Some of her patients were cremated at the Butterworth Mortuary. Eventually she moved her practice south to Olalla, Washington to land a former patient bequeathed to her. She opened her own sanitarium with a crematorium on site. Her natural healing center was named Wilderness Heights. Locals referred to it as "Starvation Heights."

Northwest author Gregg Olsen wrote a book about Linda Hazzard. He used the moniker her sanitarium earned as the title of his book, *Starvation Heights*. In it, he details the care two English women received while patients of Doctor Hazzard.

One of her patients, Claire Williamson, weighed under fifty pounds at the time of her death. Olsen writes, "After the autopsy, Claire's diamond rings were slipped from her emaciated fingers and put into Linda Hazzard's jewelry box. Her gowns found their way into the doctor's wardrobe. The victim's gold fillings and crowns were pulled from her teeth and sold to a local dentist." [11]

One of Doctor Hazzard's first victims in Seattle was the mother of Ivar Haglund. He went on to open a popular restaurant, Ivar's Fish and Chips. It is estimated that more than forty patients died in her care.

[11] Olsen, Gregg. *Starvation Heights*, NY, NY: Three Rivers Press, 2005.

I participated in a fundraiser for the Kitsap County Library System that took place at Linda Hazzard's former property in Olalla, Washington. Alongside Greg Olsen & members of the Washington State Paranormal Investigators, I gave tours of the grounds. We raised over $20,000. I gave tours of the former crematorium area. Mainly just the remnants of a building foundation, the land did have the crematorium still on site. The weight of the crematorium's furnace had caused it to sink into the ground. What we were walking around was the chimney & portions of the furnace. In the ground surrounding the chimney was grey chalky earth matter. Vines & weeds were interwoven with what, we assumed, were the remains of her many patients.

The Butterworth Mortuary opened its First Avenue entrance in 1904. The building has two original stories below First Avenue. The street was filled in and lifted over twenty feet in the regrade. Today, in the two original stories below, is Kells Irish Pub. They have an entrance on Post Alley. They have had a relatively peaceful tenure there. They routinely sprinkle the entire restaurant with holy water. The Pub was featured on an episode of Ghost Adventures but most of the ghostly events happen on the First Avenue side at 1921 First Avenue.

In the 1980s, a French restaurant, Café Sophie, opened at 1921 First Avenue. The chef was a good friend to my father and often visited our house. He would entertain my brother and me with ghost stories from the restaurant. He described chairs hovering, plates breaking, lights swinging, and a general feeling of unrest inside the building. His experiences in the building, and as the chef for the restaurant, culminated with seeing what he described as a "legion of the dead" all marching together. On that night, alone in the restaurant, he was on a ladder changing a light bulb when he saw a procession of people walk through the ladder. He described them as people of different races and eras. The spirits were walking in unison toward the back of Café Sophie. That was the night he quit.

After Café Sophie closed, Avenue One opened. The owner knew of the ghostly events, so he invited a shaman to cleanse the restaurant. For

1921 First Avenue, Butterworth Mortuary archway. Photo by Jay Lindberg.

almost two years there were no incidents. Then one afternoon, according to patrons, wine bottles shot out and flew across the restaurant, crashing to the floor. Avenue One closed soon after. Fire and Ice, an Asian restaurant, attempted to occupy the space. They were gone within seven months. No one knows exactly what happened. They held a seven year lease and had rebuilt the entire restaurant. The restaurant remained dark for many months until a group of investors bought the lease and reopened.

As of this writing, The Starlite Lounge was the last restaurant to operate in the First Avenue side of the mortuary. It closed within two years. By the time it closed, in 2007, employees said that they could hear multiple voices coming through the kitchen walls.

From an article in the *Seattle Post Intelligencer*, regarding the sudden closing of the Starlite in October 2007, "The latest casualty at 1921 was the hip eatery Starlite Lounge, which closed this year. What ultimately doomed the new restaurant was shaky management, say those in the industry. But rumor has it specters floating inside the stone and brick building - once home to a bustling death business - banged pots of disapproval to speed up moving day." [12]

Each restaurant states that they closed because of financial hardships. What caused those hardships is interesting to me. Each restaurant had plates, glassware, and bottles of alcohol that moved of their own volition and broke, depriving owners of profit and causing unexpected financial burdens. Nightly events such as those come with a high price tag.

Even more disturbing, customers complained of seeing the lower halves of bodies running through the restaurants. Former waiters from each restaurant say that a ghostly woman could been seen standing at the bar and staring at people. Patrons would request that she stop staring at them.

One day, sitting at the bar of the Starlite for a late lunch, I watched a shot glass move on its own and fall to the ground. I expected the bartender to

---

[12] Jamieson JR, Robert L. "Eateries may be cursed, or just haunted" *Seattle PI*, October 29, 2007.

Undertakers tile, 1977. Seattle Municipal Archives.

turn and be surprised by this event. However he only looked over his shoulder and continued idly talking with someone at the end of the bar. That day, I was meeting with the owners of the Starlite Lounge to tell them what I knew about the space. They were very interested in the history of the building and wanted to make the reputation of it being a haunted location work in their favor. They were even considering menu items that hinted at the history. They told me that things fell from the shelves repeatedly.

There are three doors at the front of the mortuary with ornate tile work below and more tiles on the sides of the building's entranceway. The doors are set back and a canopy of grey stone creates archways that meet the sidewalk. It's an impressive entrance for the early 1900s. The doors have brass fixtures and the center door has a handle that is in the shape of a fish. These fine details express the wealth and refinery the Butterworths must have achieved in Seattle as the city's undertakers. Gone today are the original large tiles that were in the sidewalks bearing the words "Butterworth" and "Undertakers."

In 2007, after the Starlite Lounge closed, the front of the mortuary felt cold and vacant. I would approach the entrance and point out the details in the old tiles that were not visible when the restaurant had its patio out front. Each door has a word in tiles at the base of it: to the left, "Private" in the center, "Office" and to the right, "Chapel."

One night, I was pointing out these details when suddenly a young woman taking the tour began to weave back and forth. Within seconds she fainted next to one of the stone archways. Her friends quickly picked her up and escorted her to Sonya's, a bar next door. I asked if they wanted medical assistance, but they said no. Instead we brought her orange juice. She seemed to recover as quickly as she went down. I assumed that it could have been low blood sugar or a medical condition they all knew about.

Then two days later, it happened again. This time it was a Spanish exchange student who was standing in the same location. He fainted in front of the entire group. We helped him up and he was speaking gibberish. When we brought him to Sonya's and sat him in a chair, again he recovered within seconds and appeared normal. Nonetheless, I followed the same procedure as I had two nights before, asking if he needed medical assistance and getting him a glass of orange juice.

Penny, a good friend who was giving tours with me during this time, confirmed that, on her tours, people were complaining of feeling light headed and queasy in the same location. For part of the Halloween 2007 season, the ghost tour suspended visits to the mortuary.

1921 First Avenue is on the National Historic Registry, so while the leases may change, there are architectural elements that remain the same. The balconies are exposed in the main room and an ornate etched glass wall stands where the entrance to the chapel once was. Bodies on display in the mortuary chapel were shown in a variety of ways. Spiritualism was a popular religion in the United States throughout the late 1800s and into the 1900s. In some Spiritualist funerals, bodies were made to look lifelike and they were shown seated in chairs with their eyes open.

The private balconies above the chapel provided a viewing area for the family and a podium from which a minister could speak to those in attendance. The deceased were shown below on the main level of the chapel.

Handling dead bodies in the early 1900s was a task that required patience and care. Without modern means of transportation, families of the departed would have to travel great distances by train or horse to attend a funeral. Embalming was an essential stage in preparing the bodies for viewing. According to urban legend, the Butterworth Mortuary had a pipe that ran from their embalming room to the waterfront below, to drain blood from the bodies directly out to Puget Sound.

During the Klondike Gold Rush, murder and graft became a large problem for the city. According to the book, *Cemeteries of Seattle*, "During the gold rush of the late 19th century, many men with gold-lined pockets were robbed and killed on the streets of Seattle and then dumped into Elliot Bay." To solve this problem, King County offered money for bodies: "$50 to any funeral director who would pick up and dispose of these bodies properly." [13]

This large sum of money was easily shared with able-bodied citizens. The number of murders in the city only increased because of the offer. Seattle's piers and deep tidewaters provided the perfect stage for murder. "Knockout drops administered in saloons brought death, and the bodies were carted down to the docks and tied beneath a pier, where confederates could discover the corpses the next morning and collect the twenty-five dollars paid by the city for such finds." [14]

My parents met and married in Europe. They lived in Franco's Spain for most of the 1970s and had two children there. I was the first. The town we lived in, Altea, is on the Southeast coast of Spain.

---

[13] Shannon, Robin. *Cemeteries of Seattle:* Arcadia Publishing, 2007.

[14] McNeal, Violet. *Four White Horses and a Brass Band:* The Country Life Press, 1947.

There is a wind that blows in from the Mediterranean Sea, from the coasts of Africa, Egypt, Greece, and Italy. It lingers, whispering stories of fishermen, of religion, of families who have buried ancestor after ancestor in the soil. Small whitewashed homes cascade down from the hill Altea is built on to meet the Mediterranean below.

Altea is crowned with a blue tile roofed church. In the 1970s, there were feral cats and chickens running through the dirt and stone streets. Electricity was only in the center of town. For cooking and heating almost everyone relied on gas stored in large orange canisters outside front doors. Roofs were shingled tiles and the rains would fall so hard in the spring that pieces of tile would line the streets.

My family moved to Seattle in 1979 with $400 in our pockets. My parents chose Seattle because of the Pike Place Market. They had owned a small art studio in Altea, Studio Solstone, and had painted to get by. They also made a calendar of Altea that earned them acclaim while in Spain. The market was the natural place to try to do the same.

The first few years were tough. We visited food banks and relied on my father's family connections in the area. My grandfather was a Boeing engineer and an amateur car mechanic. He gave us our first car, a pea green Vega that barely made it up Seattle hills. My brother and I would sit with my parents on the weekends and man their small stand in the market. We assisted in the evenings, preparing their wares for the next day. They introduced a calendar of the Pike Place Market in 1982 and have been successful ever since.

People talk of having spirit guides that they call on for protection. I remember that around the age of nine, I would call on my spirit guides when I went to sleep. They were Mickey Mouse, Donald Duck, and Snow White. I had a terrible fear of being awake at 2:00 a.m., which I believed was the hour that the witches came out.

I had vivid dreams of flying and became convinced that I was leaving my body. For a time I tried to teach other children in my neighborhood to do the same. I would have them stand on top of the fence that lined our front yard. Squatting down on their feet, I would then instruct them to jump off while flapping their arms. I don't recall how I came up with this impressive technique but I was adamant that it would produce night excursions.

When I was twelve years old, I saw my first ghost. My family had moved to Bainbridge Island. We rented a grey farmhouse on Winslow Way with apple trees and a large garden in the yard. The house itself was old and in disrepair. The bathtub sank into the floor and there was a slight lean to the entire first floor.

My bedroom was on the second floor above a small room that looked out on the street. It was there that I saw the ghost of an older Japanese woman sitting at the window looking out. At school, Keri, a girl who had lived in the house before we did, would ask me if I had seen the ghost. Both she and her mother had seen the same woman many times. My father also saw her frequently.

At the same time I started studying Japanese and I excelled at the language. I studied the language for the next eight years and considered getting my college degree in Japanese. Strangely enough, after my family moved out of the farm house, I lost interest in the language and lost most of what I had learned very quickly. I have wondered if the ghost of the old woman and my studies were related.

In the early 1900s, throughout the United States, Spiritualism was a very popular belief system. At the center of the religion is the role of the medium, who acts as a link between the physical and spiritual worlds. Some early séances were staged and were full of strings and lights that the medium controlled.

The magician Harry Houdini challenged such mediums and brought their trickery to light. In the 1920s, he publicly tested many famous mediums and exposed them as frauds. Before his death he stated that if anyone could communicate beyond death, he would be able to and he left a coded message for mediums in the future. Only his wife, Bess, knew the secret message.

Harry Houdini. McManus-Young Collection, Library of Congress.

Since his death on October 31, 1926, séances have been held annually on Halloween night trying to contact Houdini. In 1929, a medium named

Arthur Ford contacted Bess with a message he received. It was a succession of words that Houdini and his wife used during mind reading acts, "Rosabelle, answer, tell, pray, answer, look, tell, answer, answer, tell," which proved to be the correct secret message Houdini had left with Bess before his death.

Proof, for me, that there is something beyond our physical existence came when I was sixteen years old. My godmother, Aunt Tish, fell into a coma. She lived in Minneapolis and was a close friend to our family. My father and I went to visit her. When I was standing by her side, I held her hand. As I did, I was flooded with words and sentences in my mind. I could hear her talk although she herself could not utter a word. I could communicate on her behalf. For me, that was proof that there is something beyond the physical body and that the spirit of a person can communicate and even outlast the physical.

The question I would often get on the tour was "What is a ghost?" It is no easy task to answer. There are so many ideas and beliefs about what ghosts are. Once you open the door to the possibility of ghosts, you have to keep a firm grip on the handle so that it doesn't fly off its hinges. "Ghost" is a term that oversimplifies many possibilities.

There are a variety of explanations for what a ghost is. A ghost can be a spirit or a soul that is trapped between worlds consciously or unconsciously. It can be a residual energy that exists in organic matter, like an imprint. Perhaps, a ghost is a demon or angel. Our concept of linear time is being questioned by modern science, so it might be possible to say a ghost is a product of time folding onto itself. A ghost might also be a disembodied spirit of someone who is still living. My father would add that a ghost is the collective being of many past lives, embodied in an iconic being that represents more than just one person.

To try to explain all of these possibilities, I will start with my definition of life. In my view, life is a series of lessons that we all universally go through. We acquire language, understanding, community, identity, and a relationship with our physical and social environment. In this process of growth from childhood to adulthood and beyond, we are heading toward something, perhaps enlightenment or perhaps the peace of mind and spirit required in dying and progressing to another place. This could mean heaven, hell, or for others, reincarnation.

Death throughout cultures and religions signifies a passing to a different world or existence. In a speech credited to Chief Sealth he said, "The dead are not powerless, Death did I say? There is no death, only a change of worlds."[15]

To make that transition, I have come to believe that it requires not getting stuck on the journey that is life. You see people all the time who are stuck. They are stuck on money, on land, on relationships, on identity, on the things that are a part of our social world. To truly end life peacefully and not be trapped in some sort of limbo, we have to be able to pass through life's transitions, learn from them, and let go. If we are unable to do this, we risk returning after death and continuing in the thing that had us stuck in life.

---

[15] excerpt, 1854 speech credited to Chief Sealth, from the column by Dr. Henry A. Smith, *Seattle Sunday Star*, Oct. 29, 1887.

That may be why many of the ghosts in the market are former workers that return to work every day. In my former apartment in the market, I had one such worker. Twice I saw a man covered in flour working in my apartment. He was the ghost of a Scandinavian baker who had a bakery in the same location. In 2007 a market security guard, Leonard, died suddenly of an aneurism. News of his death was met with surprise. The morning after his death, people within the market said that Leonard was seen at the entrance to the Soames Dunn building in his security uniform ready to open the door at 8:00 a.m., just as he had done in life. He was seen standing at the same door every morning for a week following his death.

Our minds are powerful. Imagination and desire also play a role in why people think they have seen a ghost. We have a tendency to "fill in the blanks" and to respond to our environments. Exposed wires, or a high concentration of electrical power, can make anyone's hair stand on end.

Linear time is a subject up for debate with theoretical physicists exploring theories like string theory and alternate universes. String theory allows for the possibility of eleven dimensions coexisting at the same time. Alternate Universes and black holes being the portals to other worlds may have been a thing of science fiction in the past, but are now being studied as theoretical possibilities. If they hold some basis in reality, could it be that some ghosts are simply entities living in different time periods or different dimensions?

Also up for debate is the ability of our souls to travel outside of our bodies while we are alive. The term for this is "astral projection." The conscious mind leaves the body and travels in an astral form. If this is possible, perhaps some ghosts are the energetic forms of people who are alive.

Residual energy is trapped in organic materials. The materials themselves hold imprints of events and people that interacted with them. That could be one reason the ramp in the market is constantly a place where orbs appear in photographs taken there. The wood itself contains the energy of all who passed over the ramp. It may also be one reason the ghosts inside the Alibi Room are so active. The structure itself may be what is allowing those spirits to manifest. When buildings are torn down or altered, that energy is dislodged and seems to wander such as Arthur Goodwin's ghost.

Moving graves or destroying them is also thought to be related to wandering spirits. For some Native Americans, their customs and beliefs around burial may have something to do with wandering spirits. Beliefs included burying on a hill with a view of water so that the soul could rise and wander the land. The water prevented the soul from wandering too far, the grave a place to which to return.

In the neighborhood I live in now, a woman living across the street recently lost her husband. After his death, a solitary crow started to appear in the neighborhood, seen perched on top of a telephone pole that looked directly into his wife's bedroom. Another neighbor, over at our house one night, asked if we had noticed the crow. We said that we had, and he wondered if it could be the man who had just died. The neighbor told us about his pursuits to reclaim his Native American ancestry and find peace just before he died.

An Apache elder, who was on my tour one night, told me that one of the lessons of the vision quests he gives is to teach young Apaches to be able to transfer their soul to the body of an animal, so that in death they can occupy animals and be guiding forces to the living. That the crow had the soul of my neighbor seemed like a possibility. The crow still frequently sits there. Crows, especially the raven, are often considered symbols of death. For some cultures, the crow is the holder of sacred law, the guide between different worlds.

According to a poll done by CBS News, 48 percent of Americans believe in ghosts.[16] When asked if the participants believed in life after death, the number jumped considerably. Seventy-eight percent answered yes.

Our desire to believe and to establish a common understanding is evident in our entertainment and television programming. Other

---

[16] "Poll: Majority Believe in Ghosts" *www.cbsnews.com*, October 30, 2005.

countries have nationally accepted holidays for the dead. During The Day of the Dead in Mexico, families clean graves and have celebrations in cemeteries with their dead relatives. For the Chinese, August is a month of celebration and remembrance, the Chinese Ghost Festival. The living pay respect to the dead by offering them food, money, stories, and amends. Elaborate tables outside homes and businesses offer food and "Hell Money." Resembling American or Chinese notes, burning Hell Money insures prosperity for a ghost in the afterlife. Those who celebrate the Chinese Ghost Festival believe that after death the soul enters a lower world with many stages and trials. There is no direct route to paradise.

Where the Pike Place Market opened, the native people of the region, the Duwamish, originally had a year round village along the water's edge and a graveyard above. It is probably no coincidence that one of the first settler graveyards was at Second and Stewart, the Denny Hotel

Cemetery, on land that was traditionally a Duwamish burial site. Arthur Denny, one of the city's founding fathers, would not publicly confirm or deny finding cedar caskets belonging to the tribe.

"In 1898, workers at the Denny Hotel uncovered two Indian graves, recognizable as such by the burial goods with the bodies. This discovery created a rush of treasure hunters to plunder whatever remained in the graves." Mr. Denny added that, "the graves of the settlers were removed when the graveyard was abandoned, but many of the graves had been neglected and some were not found at the time of the removals. He expected that those would still be there." [17]

The removal of bodies in graveyards was fast and furious. Graves were emptied at night and with little record. While it does not originate in Seattle, the term "graveyard shift" is in common use because of this practice. In Seattle, many men have worked graveyard shifts. Early graveyards were moved four and five times.

---

[17] Angotti, Laura. "Seattle Denny Hotel Cemetery" *HistoryLink.org Online Encyclopedia of Washington State History.*

Below the Pike Place Market, on Western Avenue, there was a surface parking lot with a wooden staircase that lead up to the Joe Desimone Bridge above. The bridge jetted out and abruptly stopped over Western Avenue. At one time it was used to link Pike Place to the Municipal Market.

Visible, for many decades, was the concrete foundation of the Municipal Market which collapsed in a fire in 1961. After the collapse, a new parking garage was built on the lot.

Municipal Market collapse 1974. Seattle Municipal Archives.

The Joe Desimone Bridge was used for linking cars from Pike Place to the parking garage. Thirteen years later, in 1974, another fire destroyed the rebuilt parking garage. The bridge remained standing despite both fires. To escape the two fires, people ran across it to safety. This has left a residual energy, an imprint in the land, still felt today. The Joe Desimone Bridge is used for day-stall tenants today. A friend of mine works at the tulip stand at the entrance to the bridge. According to her, she and her son have both been pushed down to the ground by an unseen force that comes off of the bridge toward Pike Place. Other merchants report hearing the sound of running feet below and some craftspeople will not set up on the bridge because they believe it to be haunted. There certainly is a wind that whips through that area on a winter's afternoon.

For two years, I worked part time for Claudia Kelly, a craftsperson who makes scarves in the market. Claudia is not only a merchant in the market, but has also played a very important role in its governance. She served as chair for a group called the Constituency that helps oversee market rules and regulations. On most days, I set up

Claudia's day-stall on the bridge. While I worked for her, I occasionally saw a family meet at the front of the bridge: a man, woman, and two children. They were dressed in their finest. The man wore the white collar of a preacher. They gathered at the front of the bridge with a Bible and a rosary and kneeled down around one of the tiles in the floor. There they would pray, as though the tile they were gathered around were a grave marker.

While the Joe Desimone Bridge remains the same, the area around it has changed. Now a multi use building called the MarketFront connects Pike Place Market with the waterfront below. The building sits atop the old parking lot and remnants of the Municipal Market.

Craftspeople in the market attend a roll call every morning to secure a table for the day. Many of them store their wares in lockers right below the original Starbucks on Pike Place. You can often see their carts lined up at the north entrance of the day-stalls in the morning and then packed up at night next to the craft tables.

For twenty years a man named Harvey could be seen every night pushing those carts through the arcades and across Pike Place to return them to the lockers. He was entrusted with dozens of keys and kept them attached to a large metal ring that hung around his wrist like an oversized bracelet. You could hear Harvey approaching because of the jingle of those keys and the sound of carts swaying heavily on the market tiles. Harvey was a market fixture. He wore a hat that was pulled down over his forehead, like an old time newsboy. He loved chocolate. While a man of few attachments, he was devoted to the market community. Craftspeople paid him in cash each week for his work.

Unfortunately, one night, when Harvey was pushing his carts across Pike Place, he was brutally assaulted. It was a random attack that left him beaten on the cobblestones. Two market workers encountered him and took him to Harborview Medical Center. He recovered from the injuries but something had changed in Harvey. His pride was still there but his soul was injured. He died the next year.

After his death it was discovered that he had his own set of keys, to his own locker, where he often slept. When that locker was opened there were stacks of books, a sleeping bag, and bags filled with a discovery that was astonishing.

The Seattle Times wrote an article about the discovery: "A cranky, reliable enigma Harvey, who for 20-plus years pushed merchandise carts for vendors at Seattle's Pike Place Market in exchange for tips, died in April. The cantankerous but reliable worker left behind memories and mysteries, including a stash of plastic and paper bags filled with the bills he'd collected throughout the years — about $130,000 total." [18]

On the morning of Harvey's death a longtime craftsperson, who had employed him, was finishing her setup. She turned from her table and she *saw* Harvey standing right in front of her. She said, "Harvey what are you doing here, you are supposed

[18] Marc Ramirez and Sanjay Bhatt. "Market Family Loses a Beloved Fixture" *Seattle Times*, April 30, 2010

to be in the hospital?" And, just like that, he vanished. For some reason she looked at her watch right then. It was the exact time, she later learned, when he was pronounced dead at the hospital.

Harvey is a more recent ghost in the Pike Place Market. His spirit is sensed in the north end of the day-stalls and in the lockers below Pike Place. He is not seen, he is felt. People describe feeling him in close proximity as though he were still alive and standing besides them—his spirit still devoted to his work and the community that loved him.

On Western Avenue, below the market, there is a sculpture today. Created by the artist Michael Oren, it is also intended to be an interactive piece. The Point Sculpture has three sides that meet forming a point. Below the sculpture several white crystals are embedded in stone and a bench made out of the same stone is within feet of the sculpture.

The interaction with the sculpture consists of rubbing your hands on the white crystals and placing them on the point. The tip of the stone is visibly darker after years of people doing this. Supposedly, there is an energy that is detectable when placing your hands on the point. The phenomenon has a metaphysical explanation.

Ancient cultures would mark energy centers with stone formations. Stonehenge is an example of this. Underneath the Point Sculpture it is thought that three ley lines cross. Ley lines are lines underneath the earth's surface that resonate heat and energy, detectable on the earth's surface. Where they cross is a great concentration of energy providing healing and magical powers to those who choose to harness it. Behind the Point Sculpture there is a bench for those who do not want to feel the energy. It provides a place for meditation instead.

The city of Seattle is the first city in the United States to create a map of its ley lines. The project was funded by the Seattle Arts Commission. The Geo Group, who completed the task, is currently working on a project to mark energy

The Point Sculpture.

centers in Seattle with sculptures and standing stones. According to their website, www.geo.org, their goal is to "design and build a series of environmental artworks that will be used to mark and enhance the ley line energy."

The site that has continued to fascinate me is the one where Princess Angeline (Kikisebloo), daughter of Chief Sealth, lived and died. Built into the old hillside at the base of Pike Street, close to where Western Avenue is today, was her home, a small wooden shack. She lived on the land at a time when Native Americans were forced out of the city, long-houses along the shoreline were burned to the ground, and the new city of Seattle was growing at a rapid rate.

After her death, Princess Angeline's casket was escorted through the streets of Seattle by a team of black Arabian horses, a funeral rite reserved only for men. Her image was used to advertise the city of Seattle on postcards and in print into the 1960s. At the World's Fair in 1962, the one Elvis attended,

Kikisebloo (Angeline) photo by Edward Curtis. Library of Congress.

dried apple dolls made in her image were sold as souvenirs. Edward Curtis photographed Princess Angeline for the book *North American Indian* that was published in 1907. She was his first subject and was paid $1.00 for the portrait. His subsequent photos of Angeline earned him international recognition. Her image has remained a link to a world disrupted and often misunderstood.

Angeline is Seattle's most frequently seen ghost. Stories about sightings of her ghost come from many different sources. Those who have seen her say that she has piercing blue eyes.

To some, she is considered a blessing for a long life, while to others, seeing her ghost means that you are not long for this world. In life she marked a change: the end of one world and the beginning of another in Seattle.

Her ghost is often seen close to where her shack once stood. She was reportedly seen at a wedding at Cutters Bayhouse Restaurant on Western Avenue, at the Northwest corner of the market. In the story, Angeline was seen wrapped in her iconic blanket standing among the wedding party. The father of the bride approached her to ask her to leave and as he did, she disappeared.

Her ghost has also been seen on the
Bainbridge Island ferry run but, usually disappears
about half way into the crossing. It could be that the
old mosquito fleets took a different route on their
way to the Suquamish Indian Reservation where
her father is now buried and she is simply, on a
different boat.

An employee at Golden Age Collectibles,
Steve, had a very interesting experience in the comic
book store. He stated, "One November evening
several years ago, I stepped into the back office of
Golden Age Collectables and as I entered the room,
I saw that a middle-aged Native American woman
wearing either white robes or a white blanket, was
standing in the corner. In the half-second it took for
me to register what I was looking at, she vanished."

The spirit of a Native American woman is
often seen in the lower levels of the market,
sometimes walking with a thick wooden cane or
wearing a white blanket around her shoulders. This
may be the same ghost as the one described by
Steve. Some believe this ghost is Angeline.

In 2005, I was giving the ghost tour two weeks before Halloween and I started to think that I was seeing things. Every time that I brought a group in front of the Butterworth Mortuary at 1921 First Avenue, I would see hands on the windows from inside: many of them, all dark, some with what looked like mud on them. I became terrified of taking people to the building and talking in front of it. I had no explanation for what I was seeing. After starting to see the hands, I would postpone my arrival at the market to give a tour until the last possible moment.

On one afternoon I was riding my scooter down from my apartment on Capitol Hill and I stopped in a coffee shop. As I walked in the door I noticed a woman sitting down at a table with a small sign placed out. It read "Psychic Readings." She greeted me with a warm smile and instead of going to the counter for a coffee, I checked my watch and hurriedly sat down across from her. One of the first things she asked me was "Have you learned the story yet?" I assumed she meant the visions I had been having and she confirmed that to be true. I told her that I hadn't and she gave me very specific instructions, "Go and sit by the Princess and she will tell you." I knew exactly to whom she was referring and I went to visit Princess Angeline's grave.

Princess Angeline rests today next to Henry Yesler's grave at Lakeview Cemetery. Her grave marker is a simple slab of unfinished granite. The inscription reads, "Born 1811, Died May 31, 1896. The daughter of Chief Sealth, for whom the city of Seattle is named, was a lifelong supporter of the white settlers. She was converted to Christianity and named by Mrs. D.S. Maynard. Princess Angeline befriended the pioneers during the Indian attack upon Seattle on January 26, 1856."

On the morning that I visited her grave, it was a cold day and sitting at the base of the granite marker I could feel the wet of the grass through my tights. I sat for a while and looked past her grave to the hillside she is buried on, and the many markers around. I imagined for a moment that the graves were beds in which souls slept. They would soon wake up and explain why I was there. The hands I was seeing in the mortuary windows came to symbolize all the different cultures that congregated on Puget Sound before the market was built on top of the old hillside. One of the early trade languages used in the Northwest reflects the diversity of the area. The Chinook Jargon included words from Native American, English, European and Asian languages.

Angeline's story is one way to illustrate the change of worlds that occurred along Puget Sound. Coll Thrush does an eloquent and thorough telling of Native American history in Seattle and Princess Angeline's story in the book, *Native Seattle*. He writes simply, "Kikisebloo's life had been Seattle's Indian history writ small." Now when I think of her story I keep in mind the early change of worlds along the shores of Puget Sound and the continual struggle of the Duwamish tribe for federal recognition of the *The Point Elliot Treaty*.

In the 1850s, as Seattle was being settled and the population swelled, land became an issue. The Territorial Governor, Isaac Stevens, was assigned as Chief of Indian Affairs and began negotiating treaties with local chiefs. Bill Speidel in his book, *Sons of the Profits*, comments on the monumental task with irony: "Stevens was charged with the business of removing some 30,000 Indians from land they had come to believe was their own after several centuries of occupation." [19]

One of the biggest problems with Stevens' negotiation tactics was that he would sign the names of chief's himself without their being present. He also pitted tribes against each other. His choices and already growing hostilities on both sides led to a series of wars called the Treaty Wars. Little is written about the tragedies and massacres that happened throughout the state of Washington in the years 1855 and 1856. There are some personal journals that survive today and a book Ezra Meeker wrote called, *Pioneer Reminiscences of Puget Sound*. In the latter half of his book titled, *The Tragedy of Leschi*, he wrote about the relationships between settlers and the native populations. His book is one that details the injustices of the United States

---

[19] Speidel, Bill. *Sons of the Profits*, Seattle, WA: Nettle Creek, 1967.

government as people were forced onto inhospitable lands.

Ezra Meeker wrote, "The system as applied to these Indians was positively vicious, cruel and unnecessary, and if rigidly applied was certain to bring trouble." [20] This quote referred to the practice of placing several tribes, and specifically historical enemies, on the same reservation lands.

During the Treaty Wars, one chief who played a significant role in defining the conflict was Chief Leschi. His protests of the *Medicine Creek Treaty* and the deaf and hostile ears they were addressed to sparked the battles of 1855 and 1856. Charged with the murder of a soldier, Chief Leschi, who was miles away at the time of the murder, was executed for the alleged crime in a remote field in 1858. The executioner stated publicly that he felt he was hanging an innocent man. In 2004, Leschi was given a fair trial and exonerated in an unanimous verdict. *Washington State Senate Resolution 8727* formally, "recognized the injustice which occurred

---

[20] Meeker, Ezra. *Pioneer Reminiscences of Puget Sound*, Seattle, WA: Ezra Meeker, 1905.

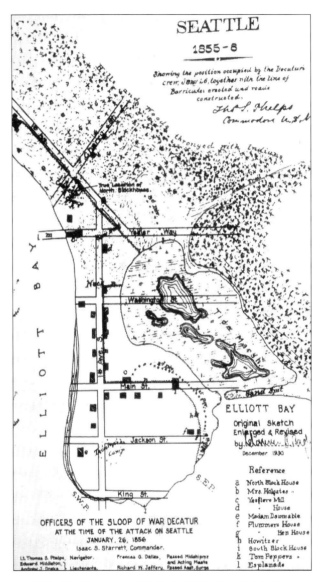

Map of Seattle drawn by T.S. Phelps. Seattle Municipal Archives.

in 1858 with the trial and execution of Chief Leschi
and honored Chief Leschi as a courageous leader
and a great and noble man." [21]

The Battle of Seattle was a one day battle
during the Treaty Wars that occurred on January
26, 1856. Princess Angeline is credited with crossing
Puget Sound in a canoe and warning settlers that an
attack by warring tribes was imminent. They
quickly ran behind the walls of an encampment
built to protect their city. They also sent word to a
ship that was docked in Puget Sound. The ship, the
Decatur, was a sloop of war of the United States
Army, equipped with canons. The crew had
received word to travel to Puget Sound in case of
such an attack.

The records kept by T. S. Phelps, Rear
Admiral in the U. S. Navy with the Decatur, provide
an eloquent account of the struggles during the
mid-1850s in Washington State.

"The early settlers, I believe, were always
kind, just and considerate in dealing with the

[21]"Nisqually Chief Leschi is hanged on February 19, 1858" *History Link Online Encyclopedia of Washington State History.*

Page 118

natives, and, so far as I know, retained to the last their friendship and good will; but as the country filled with new arrivals, many rough characters, so-called 'pioneers of civilization,' from the Western frontier and other States, appeared, who, regardless of the rights appertaining to the natives, seized their reserved lands, drove them from the fisheries, deprived them of their just dues, surreptitiously shot some, hung others, and became ingenious in their methods of oppression, until their victims, roused from the lethargy enshrouding their faculties, began to exhibit signs of discontent, yet endured patiently, hoping for a beneficial change in their condition, till the final blow to their anticipations came in 1854 with the delivery of some two hundred thousand dollars in presents, a preliminary measure on the part of the government to treaty stipulations with the tribes, which, being distributed by the agents in such a fraudulent, unjust, and outrageous manner, finally forced their eyes open to the certainties of the future, and from that moment they resolutely determined to be rid of the detestable pests fastening upon them." [22]

In a one day battle, the Decatur and the settlers fought off their attackers and reclaimed their small city. Seattle's settler population declined with fears of other attacks but within a generation, the area was filled with new arrivals. While the native population remained a visible part of the city and workforce in the area, the hostility and oppression that T.S. Phelps described in his records remained for decades.

The Barque Brontes Bakery & Cafe on Western Avenue takes its name from one of the other ships involved in the Battle of Seattle. The Map of Seattle by T.S. Phelps is on one of the walls of the cafe.

One of Seattle's first settlers, Doc Maynard, was a friend to Chief Sealth. He asked to use

---

[22] Phelps, T. S., Rear Admiral in the U. S. Navy. *Reminiscences of Seattle 'Washington Territory and the U.S Sloop of War 'Decatur' during the Indian War of 1855-1856.*

Sealth's name for the city (Seattle) and, according to legend, the Chief said no. It was the custom of his people to not utter the name of the deceased for fear they would roll over in their graves and never be at rest. Naming the city after him would condemn his soul to constant disruption. Doc Maynard devised a plan that taxed citizens in Seattle for the use of Chief Sealth's name and paid him for any future disturbances. He was also baptized in the Catholic faith. His grave in Suquamish, Washington has his Catholic name on it, Noah Sealth. If you stand at his grave and look out, you can see the entire city of Seattle from on top of the hill where he is buried.

Native Americans in Puget Sound had survived several epidemics that had devastated their populations. With the arrival of settlers in the early 1850s, more disease came: influenza, cholera, measles, and smallpox. In Seattle, the Duwamish tribe buried the dead in several locations, including the hillside where the Pike Place Market is today. Evidence of this may one day come from the land

The Viaduct 1985. Seattle Municipal Archives.

below the market, in the fill that was used to create the waterfront.

From a Seattle Post Intelligencer article about the Duwamish grave-sites along the waterfront: "They were the ancient original habitants of what is now Seattle, and there is speculation that their remains are beneath the Jell-O-like soils that lie on top of Elliott Bay and downtown Seattle. This is the newest consideration to our ongoing 'What to Do with the Alaskan Way Viaduct, Waterfront and Sea Wall' saga. Our history of disrupting sacred burial sites is well known."

It continues, "...now there is concern that there may be too much history beneath the viaduct to dig without disrupting the preserved culture of Seattle's original occupants or, worse (to most), having to stop a mega-project dead in its tracks at a substantial cost." [23]

The viaduct was an elevated highway running parallel to Seattle's waterfront. After the last major earthquake of 2001, it was judged to be unsafe and

[23] Sorbo, Cathy. "Viaduct. Cost not the only Caution" *Seattle P-I,* August 19, 2006.

in danger of failing to withstand another earthquake. With several fault lines below, that was a serious threat. Several of the proposed plans for replacing the viaduct included digging a tunnel under the Seattle waterfront. Having an archeological find, such as burial sites in the fill under the highway, could have led to many complications.

In 2004, remains of grave-sites were discovered by the State of Washington while building a bridge in Port Angeles. "About 300 graves and 785 scattered pieces of human bones have been found, along with a huge trove of ritual and ceremonial Indian artifacts, some of which date back 1,700 years."

The remains belonged to the Lower Elwha Kllalam tribe. Their ancient village of Tse-whit-zen was being unearthed daily. "In the religion of the tribe and those of many other Native Americans, disturbance of ancestral graves is a fearsome thing. It is believed that when ancestors spirits are disturbed and made restless, it may have serious consequences among the living, causing accidents, illness and death." [24]

The Native American Graves Protection and Repatriation Act protects most grave-sites when discovered. Passed into law in 1990, it requires any institution receiving federal funds to return human remains and cultural items to native peoples. In the case of the bridge, Washington State decided to abandon construction at the Port Angeles site. Members of the Lower Elwha Kllalam tribe worked alongside archeologists to remove bodies and the remains of their village.

In 2007, the tribe settled a lawsuit allowing them to rebury their ancestors on the original village site. Currently they are planning to build a museum with money awarded to them. The museum and new graveyard will stand on the eleven acres of ancestral land returned to them.

The Duwamish tribe signed *The Point Elliot Treaty* in 1855. Fifty-four thousand acres of land were given to the Territorial Government of

[24] Harden, Blaine. "Washington State Bridge Project Yields Long-Forgotten Graves" *The Washington Post*, December 19, 2004.

Washington. In exchange, the treaty provided land and money, protected fishing, hunting, and other rights. The fight for federal recognition of the treaty continues today. The *Resolution Calling for Federal Recognition of the Duwamish Tribe* reads, "we urge all members of Washington State's Congressional delegation to sponsor and support legislation to accomplish such recognition, and to notify us of their actions toward rectification of this unfortunate miscarriage of justice." [25]

In January 2009, the Duwamish celebrated the opening of a longhouse in Seattle, the first land the Duwamish have owned in a city named after their ancestral chief. It is the first longhouse in Seattle in 150 years. In April 2009, Washington State lawmakers approved the digging of a deep bore tunnel to replace the viaduct. It was completed in 2017.

No human remains were uncovered during the digging of the Seattle tunnel. Archaeologist did find some interesting

---

[25] *Resolution Calling for Federal Recognition of the Duwamish Tribe*, 46th District Democrats, January 20, 2011

things beneath the city. They found remnants of an old neighborhood south of downtown from life around 1890 to 1905. A small museum was opened as part of the massive dig, Milepost 51. It educated people about the land the viaduct was on & the early cultures that inhabited it. The museum exists online at milepost51.com.

The Market Ghost Tours began at the Gum Wall in Post Alley. It is a tucked away area below the busy market and close to the Alibi Room and Il Bistro. The Gum Wall is the exterior of the market Theater where, for the past twelve years, people have been leaving their mark with discarded brightly colored gum on the bricks. Hundreds of thousands of pieces of chewed gum cover about twenty feet of the alley. It is a favorite location for photographers in Seattle, who often use it as a setting for wedding photos.

Unexpected Productions has performed in the Market Theater since 1991. Their nightly shows draw many spectators. If attendance is low, they can

The Gum Wall.

be guaranteed that at least five seats will be filled, the ones that they reserve for every show in honor of the spirits in the building. When they rehearse, often the piano, which is to the right of the stage, will play on its own. Not a melody; just an occasional "clink, clink, clink" of the keys will be heard. Paranormal investigators have recorded the activity inside the space. Supposedly, a male and female ghost have been recorded arguing from inside the light booth. The ghost of a man has been seen walking from the north end of the building and out the door. He has been described as hurried and wearing a bowler hat.

One night after a tour, I was standing inside the theater's lobby. The door was locked. As I was talking to someone who had just been on the tour, we both noticed the door open on its own a few inches. It seemed to be pushed open from the inside and it slammed closed. Just at that moment, an actor from the theater rushed around the corner. He looked flushed and anxious. He asked if we had seen a man come by, a man in a bowler hat.

In 2010, *Darkness Radio* hosted a paranormal event in Seattle. The Ghost Adventures crew and several famous mediums and paranormal researchers were involved. I had the honor of being a guest speaker at the event. It was exhilarating. Paranormal investigations took place throughout the market. The theater was one of the sites investigated. It was a big unknown before the event. While the theater had been investigated before, we were nervous about the results. There was no reason for worry.

Of all the haunted sites investigated, the Market Theater produced the most incredible results. EVPs were clear and stated the names of actors from the theater. A voice routinely said, "I love you" during the recording sessions. For many participants they got what they wanted: seeing something with their own eyes. A dark figure was seen in the theater, casting a shadow as it went through the lobby toward the door.

The Market Theater remains an active location for paranormal activity. The ghost stories are now shared by the theater & offered as a theatrical excursion through Pike Place Market.

The Pike Place Market is a city within a city. Officials argue over policies and rules. It's a community in which individuals become iconic and add to the color of the neighborhood. It takes such characters to ensure the market's future.

In the 1980s, a group from New York City, the Urban Group, claimed ownership of the Pike Place Market and they had legal reason to do so. Through a tax incentive in which they had invested in the market, they were able to acquire ownership. It was a deal that happened behind closed doors and when it became public, cost the city over ten million dollars to correct. During that time, my father and a few other characters got on the market's roofs and by using black plastic covered the word "Public" in the neon sign that has advertised the market since the 1920s.

City council member Thomas Revelle opened the Market on August 17, 1907, with the following words. "This market is yours. I dedicate it to you, and may it prove a benefit to you and your children. It is for you to defend, protect, and to uphold, and it is for you to see that those who occupy it treat you fairly, that no extortion be permitted, and that purpose of which it was created be religiously adhered to. This is one of the greatest days in the history of Seattle, but it is only the beginning, for soon the city will have one of the greatest markets in the world."

The mission of the Market Ghost Tours was to preserve the oral tradition and people's history of the Pike Place Market and, in doing so, connect visitors to the individuals that have enhanced the market's growth. It continued: "To support the economic and social fabric of the market and educate and entertain its customers. To instill in each visitor a unique and magical relationship to the land and development of the market so that each person who hears the ghost stories is compelled to be an integral part in the future of the Pike Place Market." I hope this book has been an extension of that mission.

These ghost stories are a part of the oral tradition of the community. I am one of many tellers. The stories grow and change as they are continued to be shared. For some, the events described are as real as the cobblestones along Pike Place. For others, they are folklore and legend. Having grown up in the Pike Place Market and having been there frequently at night, I know that there is something extraordinary about it. I often look in the corners, scan the arcades, and peer down the alleys hoping for a glimpse of the souls wandering through the Pike Place Market.

Chief Sealth's grave-site in Suquamish. Photo by Michael Yaeger.

"A few more moons, a few more winters, and not one of the descendants of the mighty hosts that once moved over this broad land or lived in happy homes, protected by the Great Spirit, will remain to mourn over the graves of a people once more powerful and hopeful than yours. But why should I mourn at the untimely fate of my people? Tribe follows tribe, and nation follows nation, like the waves of the sea. It is the order of nature, and regret is useless. Your time of decay may be distant, but it will surely come, for even the White Man whose God walked and talked with him as friend to friend, cannot be exempt from the common destiny. We may be brothers after all. We will see.

We will ponder your proposition and when we decide we will let you know. But should we accept it, I here and now make this condition that we will not be denied the privilege without molestation of visiting at any time the tombs of our ancestors, friends, and children. Every part of this soil is sacred in the estimation of my people. Every hillside, every valley, every plain and grove, has been hallowed by some sad or happy event in days long vanished. Even the rocks, which seem to be dumb and dead as they swelter in the sun along the silent shore, thrill with memories of stirring events connected with the lives of my people, and the very dust upon which you now stand responds more lovingly to their footsteps than yours, because it is rich with the blood of our ancestors, and our bare feet are conscious of the sympathetic touch. Our departed braves, fond mothers, glad, happy hearted maidens, and even the little children who lived here and rejoiced here for a brief season, will love these somber solitudes and at eventide they greet shadowy returning spirits. And when the last Red Man shall have perished, and the memory of my tribe shall have become a myth among the White Men, these shores will swarm with the invisible dead of my tribe, and when your children's children think themselves alone in the field, the store, the shop, upon the highway, or in the silence of the pathless woods, they will not be alone. In all the earth there is no place dedicated to solitude. At night when the streets of your cities and villages are silent and you think them deserted, they will throng with the returning hosts that once filled them and still love this beautiful land. The White Man will never be alone.

Let him be just and deal kindly with my people, for the dead are not powerless. Dead, did I say? There is no death, only a change of worlds." [26] ~ *Chief Sealth*

---

[26] 1854 speech credited to Chief Sealth, from the column by Dr. Henry A. Smith, *Seattle Sunday Star*, Oct. 29, 1887.

BIBLIOGRAPHY

Athena. *Ghosts of Seattle*, Arglen, PA: Schiffer
Publishing, 2007.

Bruce, Robert. *Astral Dynamics*, Charlottesville, VA:
Hampton Roads Publishing Co. Inc, 1999.

Hazzard, Linda Burfield. *Fasting for the Cure of Disease*,
Seattle, WA: Harrison Publishing, 1908.

Olsen, Gregg. *Starvation Heights*, NY, NY: Three Rivers
Press, 2005.

McNeal, Violet. *Four White Horses and a Brass Band*,
Doubleday and Company, 1947.

Meeker, Ezra. *Pioneer Reminiscences of Puget Sound*,
Seattle, WA: Ezra Meeker, 1905.

Newell, Gordon and Sherwood, Don. *Totem Tales of
Old Seattle*, New York, NY: Ballantine Books, 1974.

Pierce, J. Kingston. *Eccentric Seattle*, Pullman WA:
Washington State University Press, 2003.

Phelps, T.S. *Reminiscences of Seattle Washington Territory
and the U.S. Sloop of War 'Decatur' During the Indian Wars
of 1855-1856*, Seattle, WA: The Alice Harriman
Company, 1881.

PSCA Washington. *Pioneer Square, Seattle's Oldest
Neighborhood*, Seattle, WA: University of Washington
Press, 2004.

Shannon, Robin. *Cemeteries of Seattle*: Arcadia Publishing, 2007.

Shorett, Alice and Morgan, Murray, *The Pike Place Market*: People, Politics, and Produce, Pacific Search Press, 1982.

Speidel, Bill. *Doc Maynard: The Man Who Invented Seattle*, Seattle, WA: Nettle Creek, 2003.

Speidel, Bill. *Sons of the Profits*, Seattle, WA: Nettle Creek, 1967.

Thrush, Coll. *Native Seattle*, Seattle, WA: University of WA Press, 2008.

Warren, Joshua P. *How to Hunt Ghosts*, New York, NY: Simon and Schuster Inc, 2003.

Yaeger, Antony. *Oltrano*, Bainbridge Island, WA: Rolling Bay Graphics, 1996.

Yaeger, Michael. *Insiders Tour of the Market*, Seattle, WA, Studio Solstone, 1992.

PHOTOS

Second Avenue, *Artwork of Seattle and Alaska*, 1907, W.D. Harney Photogravure Publisher, Racine, Wisconsin

The Seattle Municipal Archives:
First Avenue. Item No. 33172
Market Sign. 1973. Item No. 33150
Green Parrot. Item No. 35976
Denny Hill Regrade. Item No. 3429
Pike Place Market, 1907. Item No: 33280
The market in 1921. Item No: 33286
Tunnel under Pike Place Market. Item No: 57745
La Salle Hotel. Item No: 34896
Parking garage and bridge. Item No: 31650
Joe's Rice Bowl. 1967. Item No: 34938
Undertakers, Mortuary. Item No: 33643
Battle of Seattle map, 1855-1856. Item No: 130309
The Viaduct. 1985. Item No: 57737
Victor Steinbrueck 1965. Item No. 57709

The Library of Congress:
Princess Angeline. *Library of Congress, Prints and Photographs Division*, LC-USZ62-99663
Harry Houdini. *McManus-Young Collection*

Inside cover, Lower Post Alley. *Antony Yaeger*
Author photo. *Kristi Lloyd Photography*
Author & her father. *Lance Wagner*

HAUNTED RESTAURANTS
IN THE PIKE PLACE MARKET

THE ALIBI ROOM, serving oven fired pizzas.
Three reported ghosts.
Location: Post Alley
85 Pike Street

IL BISTRO, serving Italian food in a gorgeous
environment, a full bar perfect in the early evenings
for a quick drink. One female spirit has been
reported and the bathrooms are supposedly haunted
as well.
Location: Post Alley
93 A Pike St

GHOST ALLEY ESPRESSO, serving unique
espresso drinks. Arthur Goodwin haunts this
little shop. Several other spirits have been seen
around the shop.
Location: Post Alley
1499 Post Alley

1921 FIRST AVENUE, former mortuary, no
restaurant occupying the space at this time.
Location: 1921 1st Avenue

THE CAN CAN, an incredible vaudeville style show or music every night, a full bar and menu, located in the Underground. Formerly Patti Summers Lounge, paranormal occurrences are in the kitchen.
Location: Corner Market Building
94 Pike St

KELLS IRISH PUB, located in the former Butterworth Mortuary, Kells has a full restaurant and bar with live Irish music. A young female ghost occasionally shows herself in the pub, as well as a few other spirits, including one that dances.
Location: Post Alley
1916 Post Alley

THE PIKE PUB & BREWERY, offers a variety of international award winning beers and delicious food. Family friendly and able to accommodate large groups, "Naughty Nellie" is supposedly seen in the Pub and Brewery.
Location: The South Arcade
1415 1st Avenue
Seattle, WA 98101

JARRBAR, on Western Avenue, serves craft cocktails and tinned fish. The ghost of a man has been seen at the bar.
Location: Western Avenue
1432 Western Avenue

The author and her father. Photo by Lance Wagner.

With a glint in his eye that made a listener draw closer, my father always had a passion for story telling. For the encouragement to develop the Market Ghost Tours, I thank my father, Michael Yaeger.

This book is the culmination of many years of doing research into the ghost stories of the Pike Place Market. Using my experience as an archivist I searched through rare books and articles to substantiate the stories. I also interviewed descendants of the people written about in this book.

Writing it would not have been possible without the support & assistance of many people. Thank you to the following; Heather Chermak, Michele Lindberg, and all of the tour guides, to Sheila Lyon, Ram and Nina Menon, Antony Yaeger, Sarah Yaeger, Joanne De Pue,

Faye the Tattooed Psychic, Jay Lindberg, Bariah Brown, Jim Hinde, Claudia Kelly, D.H. Cass Magnuski, Jana Szabo, Kerry Serl, & Caleah Dean.

Also, thank you to the Alibi Room, Kells, Il Bistro, Unexpected Productions, History Link, The Seattle Public Library, PDA Security & to all the people who attended the Market Ghost Tour.

Mercedes Yaeger was the owner of the Market Ghost Tours in Seattle. Aside from her own tours, Mercedes has been a tour guide in Seattle since 1999. She was a developer on the Sub Seattle Tour and worked for the Underground Tours. Her resume includes roles in documentary film production, radio appearances, and talent with the local PBS station, KCTS9. After selling her popular espresso shop, Ghost Alley Espresso, in 2018, she now roasts coffee on Queen Anne Hill. Mercedes received a Literary Lion Award from the King County Library System in 2011 for Seattle's Market Ghost Stories.

FIND OUT MORE
ABOUT THE SUBJECTS IN THIS BOOK

www.historylink.org

www.pikeplacemarket.org

www.duwamishtribe.org

www.seattlehistory.org

www.seattle.gov/cityarchives

www.starvationheights.com

www.unexpectedproductions.org

www.pikeplacemarket.org

www.vanishingseattle.org

www.seattlewatercolors.com

www.darknessradio.com

www.greggolsen.com

www.wspir.org

www.antonyyaeger.com

www.vintageseattle.org

www.geo.org

www.milepost51.com